Sasha Gusov
took the photographs ...

Amanda Renshaw
... did the rest.

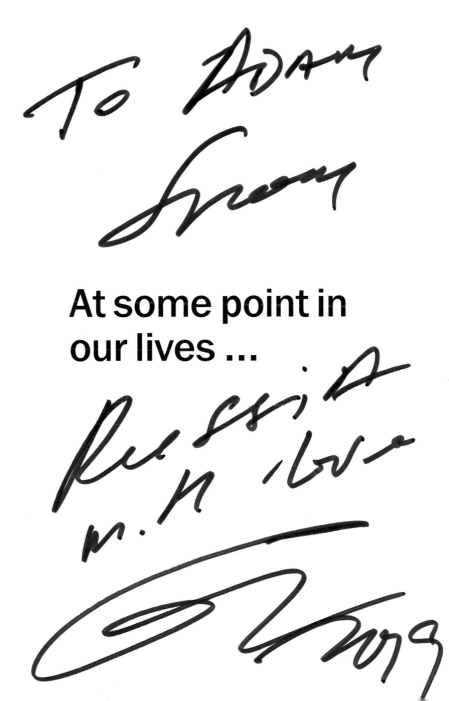

At some point in
our lives ...

… we all get the feeling the world revolves around us; that we are somehow special or unique.

Tel Aviv

We forget there are billions of other people on the planet who are …

Although we come in different
shapes and sizes ...

London

... we all experience
the same emotions ...

... pain,

confusion,

Damascus

loneliness,

Qalat Nadim

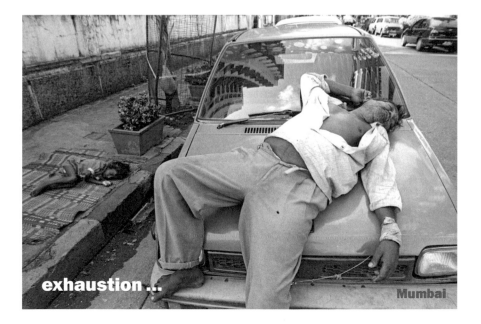

exhaustion ...

Mumbai

... and **elation!**

Almaty

Although we may
be born to different
parents and in
different cultures,
we all have attributes,
quirks and foibles
that make us human.

We care for and protect our young …

Harare

... and we continue to care for each other ...

Monte Argentario

Dead Sea

... as we grow older.

Rome

Science has proven that male and female humans are more similar than they are different.

However ...

... isn't it mostly men who lay their arms territorially over the back of the next chair ...

and sit with their knees apart?

...even when their ogling is misplaced.

London

Udaipur

Women seem to have a habit of buying underwear that's too small ...

Taganrog

... and who can explain the relationship they have with their bags?

People like us love to bask in the sun …

Zekhnovo

Rostov-na-Donu

... enjoy the water ...

... and lie on the beach.

Taganrog

The common
understanding
is that we are
evolved from
chimpanzees,
but, perhaps ...

Dead Sea

Taganrog

... seals are

Dead Sea

... a closer relative.

Those of us who enjoy lying in the sun take the process very seriously.

We need to be properly equipped, with towel, suntan lotion and other ...

Dead Sea

... essential protection.

To further enhance our time in the sun we use a selection of props.

Santa Margherita di Pula

But however many props we might invent, we've never mastered the art of gracefully changing back into dry clothes.

So it's greatly appreciated when help is at hand.

Tel Aviv

Dead Sea

Some of us love lying in the sun so much that we do it just about anywhere ...

Santa Marinella

... and the more of us doing it together, the merrier.

We enjoy the company of others and are often seen hanging out in pairs.

Mumbai

Tidworth

But we also enjoy
the company of
more than one ...

Petra

Riyadh

... and we are particularly good at doing things in larger groups.

Cuenca

This may be because we
enjoy a sense of order …

Minsk

... and discipline.

Medina

But we can also be flexible and inventive about where we do things …

London

... often choosing unpredictable locations.

Sometimes our actions are just difficult to fathom.

Echmiadzin

Our main form of communication is talking. Unlike other animals whose languages sound the same regardless of where they are born …

Bordeaux

... people like us speak many different languages and dialects.

Valencia

This means that ...

… we don't always understand what the other person is saying.

Riyadh

To be more effective we therefore often use other forms of communication.

Smiling can be popular ...

Riyadh

Jaipur

Riyadh

... and touching can be effective.

Rome

But kissing may be the most persuasive way to get one's point across.

Florence

**Every so often we are quite happy
not to communicate with anyone.**

**Time spent alone allows us to enjoy
our own thoughts without distraction
and resolve problems.**

Telephones enable us to check in with each other whenever we feel lonely or there is something important to report.

London

This seems to be just
about all the time.

Rome

Jodphur

London

Ascot

Smartphones allow us to get in touch from just about anywhere, although it's not always easy to find a signal.

Sometimes the person we are talking to is a long way away, so we have to speak up.

Kochi

Telephones have become such an important part of our lives we are loathe to be without them on any occasion.

Minsk

Barcelona

Text messages are often short and not very accurate. It often takes several to get the point across.

A single call might have been more efficient.

There are other ways we tell people things. One of them is advertising. Our world is overrun with pictures of people who don't look much like us.

London

MADISON AV

We are accosted by these images every day. They are plastered on billboards ...

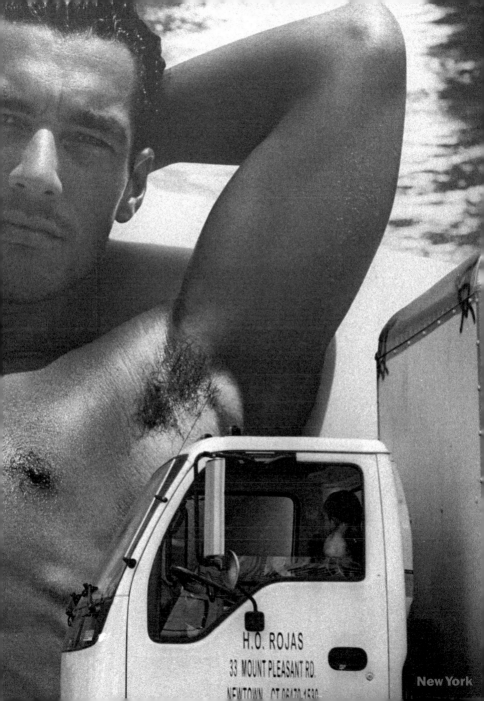

H.O. ROJAS

33 MOUNT PLEASANT RD.

NEWTOWN, CT 06470-1530

… by corporations who try to convince us that if we buy the product …

fragrance for men
CE & GABBANA
the one gentleman

... we might
actually begin
to look like the
people in the
pictures.

BRAND NEW GINA TO

PLEASE VISIT OUR STORES OU

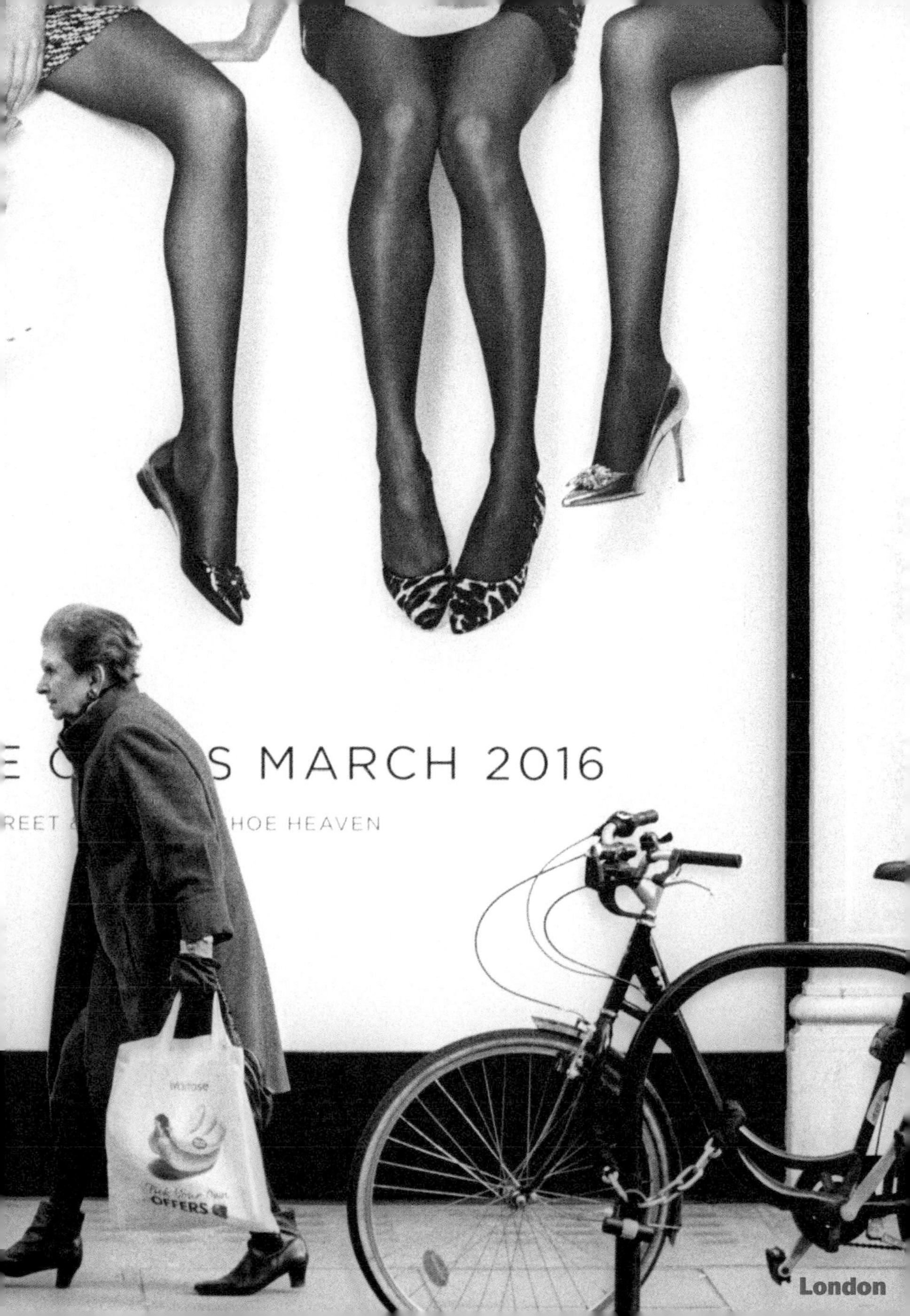

London

The chances that we will are generally very remote and, more often than not, the advertisers' promises are ...

... completely empty.

Perfect people loom over us. Out of step with reality.

London

Madrid

The posters tell us
which films to see,
which phones to buy ...

what to, or not to, eat and drink …

Vladikavka?

and who to vote for.

Victoria Falls

Once we've voted, they also tell us who our leaders are, lest we forget.

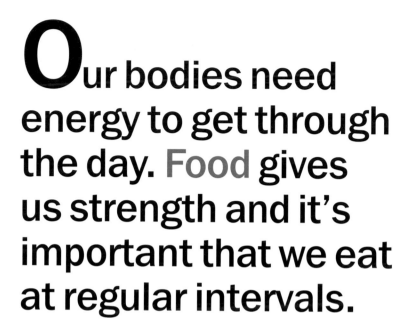

Our bodies need energy to get through the day. Food gives us strength and it's important that we eat at regular intervals.

Sometimes we eat alone...

... sometimes we eat together ...

London

Jeddah

Celebrating
Her Majesty the Queen's
Golden Jubilee

THE QUEEN'S
2002
GOLDEN JUBILEE

... and sometimes we are so hungry ...

London

... that we eat

... on the go.

Rome

People like us spend a lot of time taking photographs.

Udaipur

We learn to pose for the camera at a very young age and ...

New York

... we enjoy documenting our lives.

Rome

We might take a photograph to commemorate an important occasion.

But we also take photographs of less important events …

... each other

Santa Margherita di Pula

Yardenit

Javea

… and ourselves.

Barcelona

**Some of us take photographs
to earn a living.**

Damascus

**We might work on the street with
relatively simple tools.**

Sometimes, however,
the size of the tools
can take over.

Some non-professionals can also take photography very seriously.

We consider ourselves superior to other species. We believe that, unlike us, animals cannot imagine alternative futures or be self-reflective.

Nevertheless, we enjoy their company.

We work together ...

Mumbai

Most of us need to earn a living and we spend many of our waking hours at work.

Our forms of employment vary enormously.

Mumbai

Galapagos

Hard work is valued and rewarded.

London

Riyadh

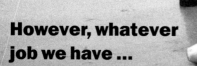

**However, whatever
job we have ...**

... the most
satisfying one
is watching
others at work.

At the end of a busy day we all need some respite.

London

When we are not working, and have time to spare, we engage in activites designed to make the time pass.

Pretoria

Valencia

These activities are played to a predetermined set of rules.

**Some of them can be more taxing
on the brain than others.**

We might try shifting a ball up and down a field with the aim of putting it into the back of a rectangular frame with a net ...

... or we might roll balls across a lawn ...

... throw a
plastic plate at
each other ...

London

… or even put ourselves into an enclosed space with a bull.

Valencia

We love being involved in the activity, but are also quite content to act as onlookers.

Many of us like to spend our free time looking at art. People often say that they don't know much about art, but they know what they like.

London

Art serves no practical function and to many of us it can be a little baffling.

In the past we sometimes bought a washing machine or coffee maker to demonstrate our wealth.

Today some of us buy art instead.

People like us are naturally curious.

We are inquisitive and ...

London

London

... intrigued by difference.

In an attempt to learn about things we don't know, we travel.

Mada'in Saleh

Our modes of transport ...

Rajasthan

... are varied.

Madurai

Bordeaux

When we arrive at our destination we often do things which are …

Fish River Canyon

Monte Carlo

London

Kronberg im Taunus

out of character ...

Ascot

... and which we wouldn't normally attempt at home.

Some of us are obliged to travel for work.
When we do, we do so in relative comfort.

London

When we do it by choice and for pleasure …

... the conditions are not always as comfortable.

London

We are thirsty for knowledge and reach for information that comes from a reliable source. We read …

... newspapers, magazines, books, and ...

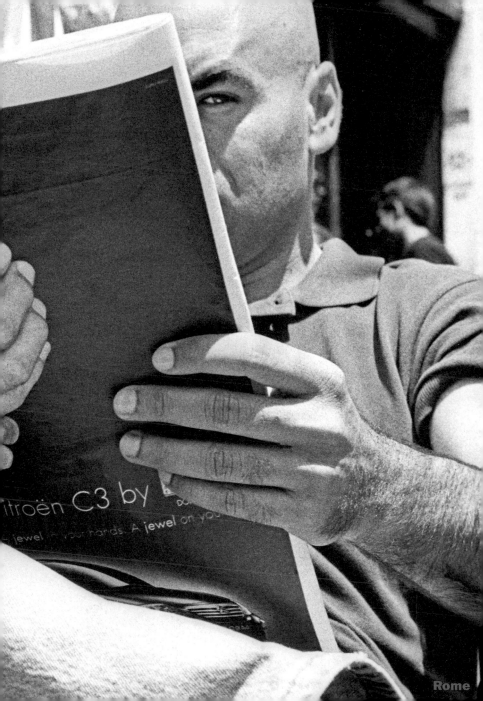

itroën C3 by

jewel in your hands. A jewel on you

Rome

... other printed matter.

Rome

Dresden

Thousands of years ago, we led a nomadic existence, surviving on what we could catch or gather. Today we depend on shops to provide the goods that feed and clothe us.

Mumbai

Shopkeepers carefully display their wares to seduce us into buying them.

We grow attached to our goods and possessions and have invented various ways of transporting them.

Istanbul

We carry small, heavy and awkward things.

Damascus

Goshavank

Baku

Bucharest

Much like ants, our burdens are often larger than we are.

Jodhpur

People like us often say that beauty is in the eye of the beholder.

London

We have wrestled with
the definition of beauty
for centuries. We find
it impossible to define
and it changes ...

... from culture to culture and generation to generation.

We want to be
attractive to
others.

Jaipur

The best way of
seeing what we
look like is to
glance in a mirror.

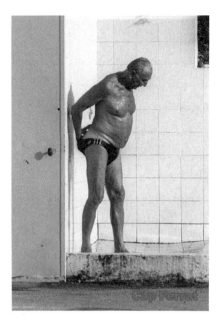

Our outward appearance is important ...

Valéncia

and we take great care with
our wardrobe ...

Tidworth

always finding the outfit that conveys …

London

Victoria Falls

London

the image we want to project.

Monte Carlo

We can also improve the way we look by keeping our bodies in trim.

Staying fit can also make us live longer. So some of us commit an enormous amount of time ...

Victoria Falls

... and effort to our exercise regime.

London

ACCESO
MINUSVALIDOS

USE PAPELERAS

Sometimes it may feel like an uphill struggle.

But we know that a healthy body equals a healthy mind and, more importantly, a healthy body can help attract a mate.

So we persevere, until ...

... we get the exercise right.

Tel Aviv

B
eing like us is a strenuous business. The challenges that we encounter on a daily basis wear us out, and …

Harare

... rest is essential.

Whatever culture we are from and whoever our parents may be, rest repairs our strength, regulates our moods and restores our minds …

Rome

so we do it wherever we can ...

London

Damascus

until we are refreshed …

Eastbourne

... and ready to start all over again.

Photographer's acknowledgments.

I am indebted to the many people
who have graciously served
as actors in my human comedy
(of which I am also a part). I am
also grateful to those who have
provided essential support,
without which these photographs
and this book would not be
possible. My sincere thanks go
to Almaly Assets Management
Company for their ongoing
generosity; to Irina Novitskaya and
Evgenia Khaldey for their kindness
and encouragement, to Peter
Davenport, Kara Hattersley-Smith,
Molly Syrett and, of course ...
... to Anna, for keeping me sane.